Charlie's War Illustrated

REMEMBERING WORLD WAR ONE

My grandfather always wore a poppy in his buttonhole on Remembrance Day. When I asked him why, this is what he told me . . .

Mick Manning & Brita Granström

FRANKLIN WATTS

Before the War

I was born in 1893 and it was a very different world to the one we live in today. It was still the age of the horse and carriage; cars were as rare as hen's teeth and planes hadn't even been invented. I had seven brothers and sisters and, although we didn't have much money, we were a happy bunch.

OGDEN'S

STARLING.

Mum kept hens for eggs and Sunday dinners. I also caught wild birds in the garden to add to her pies; and brown trout in the stream, too.

He likes pear-drops ...

... that'll make up for the bites!

I caught the rats in my aunts' shop with my bare hands. I got paid in sweets and I shared them with my younger brother Fred – we were pals!

Our dad, Percy, had come from a well-to-do London family but he was orphaned as a boy. He'd moved to Sheffield and found work as a clerk in the steelworks. He married a shopkeeper's daughter called Emma Salmon. They named me Charles Muss after my grandfather.

I left school when I was 12 and got a job at Vickers Steelworks. Here I am with my workmates.

But life would soon change forever – war was on its way.

In 1914 Franz Ferdinand, the heir to the throne of Austria-Hungary, was shot by a Bosnian Serb. That sparked an argument that had been brewing for ages and turned into World War One. Countries all over the world chose sides: the Central Powers (Germany, Austria-Hungary, Turkey and Bulgaria) fought against the Allies (including Britain, Australia, Canada, New Zealand, France, India, Belgium, Russia and Japan). Italy joined the Allies in 1915 – and the USA in 1917.

You had to be over 18 to join the Army. Fred lied about his age because he'd only just turned 17. Mum cried her eyes out when she found out, but it was too late; we'd both signed up for King and country. We had joined the Royal Field Artillery — the lads who manned the field guns on the front line.

18? Well if you say so. Sign here lad!!

Those Germans are monsters, lads!

Joining Up, 1914

In 1914, war broke out. It was Fred who spotted the poster first! Lord Kitchener seemed to be pointing right at us! When we went into the recruiting office to enlist, it was packed with blokes: shop assistants, factory workers, office boys . . . We all wanted to be soldiers; we all wanted to be like the red-coated war heroes from the *Boy's Own Paper*.

Field-Marshal Earl Kitchener.

Hats off to the Flag
we all love and adore,
And give it a mighty
great cheer,
For with gallant Commanders
like this to the fore —
Old England has
nothing to fear.

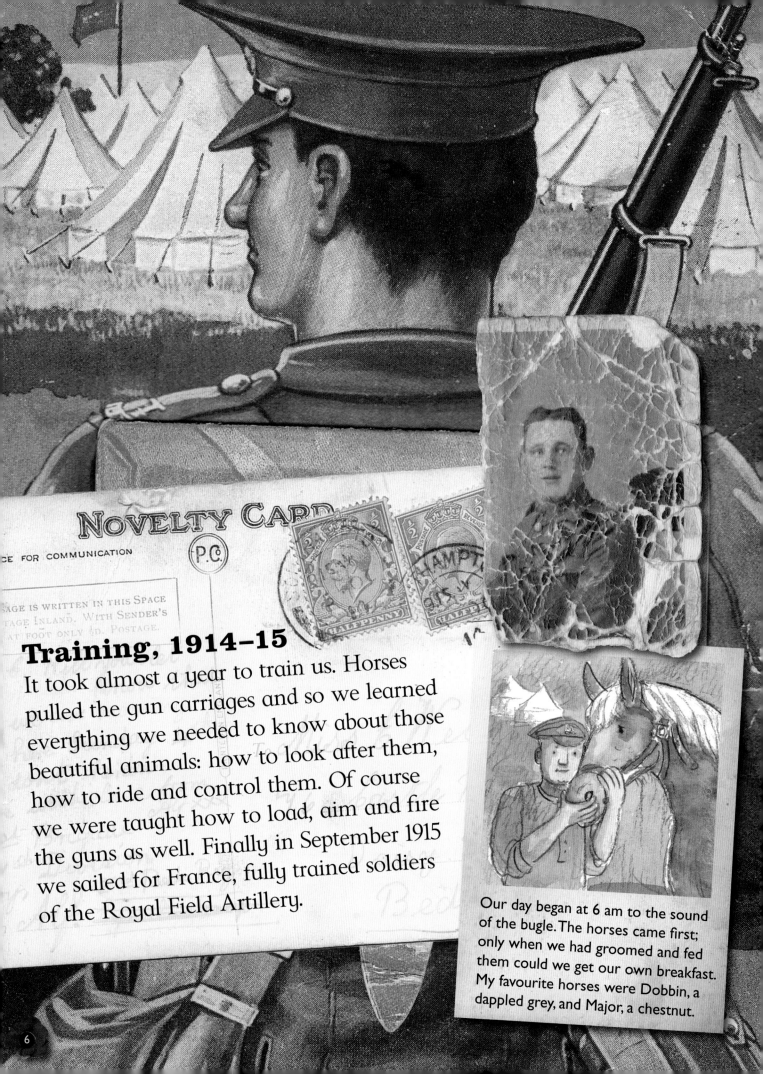

NOVELTY CARD

P.C.

CE FOR COMMUNICATION

SAGE IS WRITTEN IN THIS SPACE
TAGE INLAND. WITH SENDER'S
AT FOOT ONLY ½D. POSTAGE.

Training, 1914–15

It took almost a year to train us. Horses pulled the gun carriages and so we learned everything we needed to know about those beautiful animals: how to look after them, how to ride and control them. Of course we were taught how to load, aim and fire the guns as well. Finally in September 1915 we sailed for France, fully trained soldiers of the Royal Field Artillery.

Our day began at 6 am to the sound of the bugle. The horses came first; only when we had groomed and fed them could we get our own breakfast. My favourite horses were Dobbin, a dappled grey, and Major, a chestnut.

Gun Drill taught us how to load, aim and fire the different guns, including 18-pounders and 4.5-inch Howitzers, 'at the double'.

I was promoted to Bombardier and appointed as a 'layer' – the one who sights and aims the gun.

An artillery brigade usually had three batteries. Each battery had six field guns and around 200 men including: officers, a sergeant-major, quartermaster, trumpeters, sergeants, corporals, bombardiers, gunners, drivers, saddlers, wheelwrights and blacksmiths.

Halt! Action right!

gun crew

drivers

gun   limber

The gun and ammunition carriages were known as 'limbers' and pulled by teams of six horses. Three men rode the pairs of horses to steer them and look after them.

CARD

France, 1915

There were crowds waving when we steamed into the French port. We felt like heroes! Next day, travelling along French country lanes, we passed a column of German prisoners. They stared blankly up at us as we towed our gun limbers along that road, a road that was taking us towards the distant sound of big guns and the Battle of Loos . . .

For most of us young lads, France was our first visit to another country. When we got off the boats, crowds of French people waved and cheered and bands played. It made us all feel important and brave.

THE FRONT LINES

Western Front
(1915) (1918)

Sheffield
Liverpool
UK
RMS Lusitania
sank here
7th May 1915
GERMANY
RUSSIA
Ypres • Passchendaele
Loos • BELGIUM
The Somme • LUXEMBOURG
Verdun
FRANCE
SWITZERLAND
(Neutral)
AUSTRIA-
HUNGARY
SERBIA
ROMANIA
ITALY
BULGARIA
TURKEY
(The Ottoman Empire)
Salonika • • Gallipoli
GREECE
ALGERIA
PALESTINE
Jerusalem • • Damascus
Gaza •
Salonika Front
(around 1917-18)
*The Salonika Front was
known as 'The Birdcage'*
TUNISIA
Suez Canal
LIBYA
EGYPT
*Allied advance into
Palestine 1917-18*

World War One was fought on several different fronts around the world. The front lines moved backwards and forwards as the different sides gained or lost land. Fred and I were to fight on three of them; the Western Front, Greece and Palestine (moving in from Egypt). They are shown on this map.

The Germans don't look like monsters to me. They're just like us!

WAR DIARY
or
INTELLIGENCE SUMMARY.
(Erase heading not required.)

of 117th Brigade R.F.A.   Army Form C. 211

Instructions regarding War Diaries and Intelligence
Summaries are contained in F. S. Regs., Part II.
and the Staff Manual respectively. Title pages
prepared in manuscript.

Summary of Events and Information

Remarks and
references to
Appendices

Salonika, 1915

But Loos wasn't for us! After more training around the River Somme we were ordered to the port of Marseilles to embark for Greece and the Salonika Front. We arrived at a camp some joker had called 'Happy Valley'. But it was no Greek holiday! We endured snow blizzards so cold that men lost fingers and toes to frostbite; then, when the summer arrived, it became feverishly hot. A hard time we had of it fighting the Bulgarian Army in those hills.

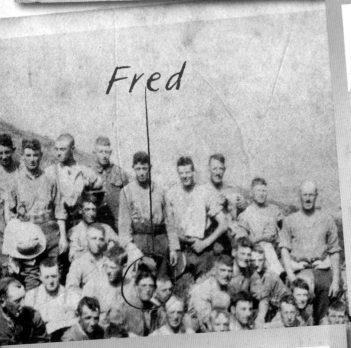

Fred

It wasn't just the British fighting the Central Powers in the Mediterranean. There were ANZACs (Australian and New Zealand troops), Indians and French and they had had a bad time of it at Gallipoli in Turkey. The Salonika Front was set up to protect Serbia, one of the Allies.

Me

We weren't only fighting human enemies in the hills of Greece. There were waterborne germs that spread typhoid fever and dysentery and Salonika's blood-sucking mosquitos carried malaria, so our officers made us take a bitter medicine called quinine every day – ugh!

Drink this, Frank.

Hospital Ship, 1916

Half a million soldiers were treated for illnesses and non-battle injuries in Salonika. I found myself alongside injured comrades on board HMHS *Rewa* sailing for England. The clever nurses looked after us all very well and I spent six weeks in a Liverpool hospital.

Egyptian Expeditionary Force, 1917

Next, I was ordered to join a new brigade sailing for Egypt. I saw pyramids there and had my first taste of watermelons; I even had a go at sitting on an Aussie soldier's camel - what a laugh! But it was no picnic; we crossed the baking desert to fight for a year in the dust and sands of Palestine. Then, after capturing Jerusalem from the Turkish Army, we were shipped back to the mud and blood of France . . .

We're Aussies from the Imperial Camel Corps!

Ouch! That tattoo needle stings!

Any free time was spent sightseeing or exploring the local towns. There were theatres, clubs and tattooists young lads like us were keen to visit.

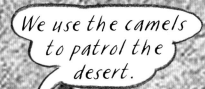

We use the camels to patrol the desert.

My old brigade from Salonika had also been transferred to Palestine so I was reunited with Fred and other mates.

KABOOM!

The Allies had set up the Egypt Expeditionary Force to protect their ships coming through the Suez Canal into the Mediterranean. Then they began to move into Palestine, fighting the Turkish Army at Gaza and Beersheba. A lot of mates of mine died as we fought to liberate Jerusalem.

On the Western Front, 1918

Back in France, we moved our guns into position behind the trenches and the slaughter began again. Between the fighting, there was a lot of hanging around. Many of us got infested with lice that made us itch like crazy. We killed them by running a candle flame over our blankets and uniforms until we heard them go 'pop' in the heat! Another problem for some lads was 'trench foot'; days in wet boots and socks made their feet go rotten.

If you stuck your head over the top of a trench, you risked getting shot by a sniper so we used periscopes to peep over the edge.

We'd sing silly songs about the terrible things that were happening to us. It helped!

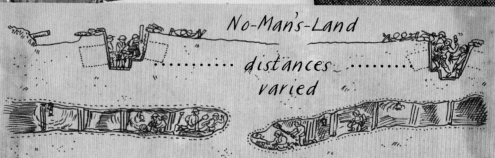

On the Western Front, the Allies and Central Powers had dug defensive trenches facing each other across No Man's Land. Both sides carried out night raids, sniping, shelling and full-scale attacks. Sometimes one side dug a tunnel under their enemy's trenches and filled it with explosives.

Cheers!

Once, billeted in some bombed-out buildings, I found a cellar full of champagne bottles. We'd never tasted it before and we swigged it like fizzy pop – but it soon made us very sick. We got into trouble; our officer fined us a week's wages!

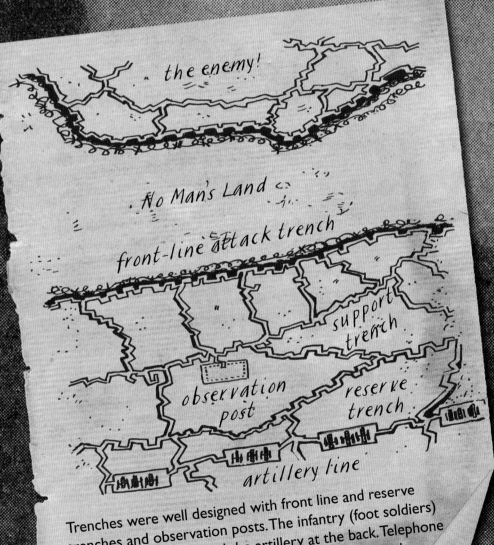

the enemy!

No Man's Land

front-line attack trench

support trench

observation post

reserve trench

artillery line

Trenches were well designed with front line and reserve trenches and observation posts. The infantry (foot soldiers) were in the trenches and the artillery at the back. Telephone wires ran along the ground keeping everyone in touch.

Gas

We soon found out about a silent weapon, poison gas. Our battery had been taught what the different sorts could do: choke you to death, give you terrible skin burns or cause temporary blindness. Some gas smelled like the pear-drop sweets I used to get from my aunties' shop and I've never eaten them since! The day we took up position on the front line we saw a column of men, blinded by gas, being led to safety. They were singing to keep their spirits up . . .

We fought the Second Battle of the Somme, at Bapaume, and the battles along the Hindenburg Line before finally beginning to feel we might win the war. During one battle, Fred saved a wounded man by sharing his gas mask. Fred developed breathing problems in later life because of that act of bravery.

The number of casualties on the Western Front was horrifying. During the first Somme offensive in 1916 the British suffered 60,000 casualties in just the first day. At the Battle for Passchendaele in 1917 the Allies captured five miles of battlefront at a cost of 140,000 lives; roughly two soldiers were killed per inch of ground gained. In total around 9 million troops were killed and 20 million wounded in World War One.

Picture cards

Swapping the colourful picture cards from cigarette packets took our minds off things. Fred and I collected them on our travels. German planes were my favourites; it still amazed me that people had learned to fly. Sometimes we saw the real planes, like angels in the sky above our lines. But they were angels of death, cos they reported us and our gun positions to their own artillery . . . then we'd get a real pasting!

Tanks were a British invention originally called 'water tanks' to keep them top secret from the enemy. When first used in battle they were a deadly surprise to the enemy. But they were a danger to the men inside too because they soon filled with poisonous engine fumes.

A TRIBUTE TO THE TANKS

A TRIBUTE TO THE ROYAL NAVY (SUBMARINES)

Both sides had submarines. German U-boats sank many ships. They mainly targeted supply ships, including American boats crossing the Atlantic. The USA didn't like that . . .

DREADNOUGHT.

HMS *Dreadnought* was a famous British battleship launched in 1906 with turbo steam engines and powerful guns. Many countries, including America and Germany, built their own versions of 'dreadnoughts'.

German zeppelins were airships and they looked like huge, sausage-shaped balloons. They could fly long distances and drop bombs.

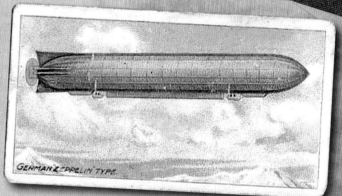

GERMAN ZEPPELIN TYPE.

The Trenches

One day, during the Second Battle of the Somme, Fred got sent to the front-line trenches to help repair our damaged telephone wires. These cables snaked from our battery to the front-line observation post and were often broken by enemy artillery explosions. Fred made it back, but for days he talked of muddy trenches, wounded men, waterlogged shell holes and a smell in the air like rotten meat . . .

We had a hard time in the artillery but we were glad not to be in the infantry.

In the trenches, food was rationed, mainly tinned and not very nice. One memo sent to the troops said: 'Don't be surprised if there is no pork in your tins of pork and beans, the pork has been absorbed by the beans.'

It wasn't all gloomy; some blokes told jokes and sang funny songs, others played cards or carved 'trench art' from bits of wood.

Barrage action, 1918

Our officers would get their orders from either HQ or the front-line observation post. Often the order was to open fire on trench raiders, or enemy supply columns, but before any 'big push' we had to pound the enemy with a day and night barrage. We tried to clear a path ready for our infantry's advance. Our orders: 'Cut their barbed wire! Destroy their defences! Smash their artillery!' Of course, they fired back. We nicknamed some enemy shells 'whizzbangs'.

Instructions regarding War Diaries, Parts
Summaries are contained in F. S. Regs.
and the Staff Manual respectively. Title pages
will be prepared in manuscript.

Summary of Events and Information

Place   Date 1915   Hour

#333   Wt. W2544/2454 700,000 5/25 D. D. & L.   A.D.S.S./Forms/C. 2118.

"We have to move these guns fast."

"Come on, Dobbin!"

If we came under fire, we had to be ready to hitch up our guns 'at the double' so we could move to new positions.

"Faster, lads!"

Many women worked in the dangerous ammunition factories back home. Sometimes we found a message or a photo in the boxes of new shells asking for a 'pen pal'.

♪♪ *Hush here comes a whizzbang, and it's making right for you! You'll see all the wonders of No Man's Land, if a whizzbang hits you!* ♪♪

All the ammunition and supplies had to be brought in by packhorses. It was a dangerous job. Many men and horses were killed by enemy fire; some even drowned in deeply flooded shell holes.

A TRIBUTE TO THE ROYAL ARTILLERY

23

Over the top

Just before the infantry went into battle we'd cease firing. In the hush that followed we'd listen to the larks singing and hope we'd hit our targets. Then the sounds of battle would begin again . . . All along the front line we'd hear officers blowing whistles, the signal for the infantry to attack. Tough lads, shy lads, mummy's boys and bullies pushed out of the trenches in their thousands; going 'over the top' into a storm of bullets and explosions.

TRIBUTE TO THE RED CROSS

TO THE R.A.M.C. FIELD AMBULANCE

Stretcher-bearers and medics collected the dead and wounded. They worked in pairs as bodies were heavy and needed gentle handling. It took four of them to carry a stretcher over battlefield obstacles or mud, often under enemy fire.

Machine gunners fired 500 bullets a minute in criss-cross paths into the crowds of advancing soldiers.

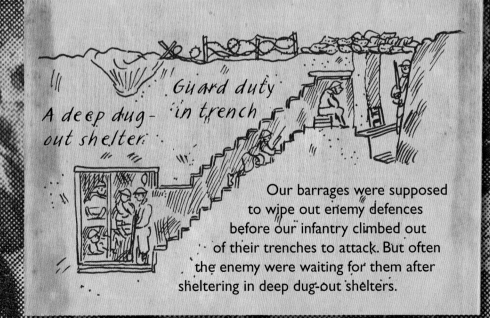

A deep dug-out shelter

Guard duty in trench

Our barrages were supposed to wipe out enemy defences before our infantry climbed out of their trenches to attack. But often the enemy were waiting for them after sheltering in deep dug-out shelters.

Letters home

Letters and postcards were the only way we could keep in touch with our loved ones. The army always censored our letters first, removing facts such as place names or other details that might be useful to the enemy, by drawing a thick black line ~~then there would be a thick black line through~~ like this to make the sentence unreadable.

To my dear Mother

Hope and Love

These lovely silk postcards were made by women in France and Belgium and they became very popular with the troops.

OFFICIAL PHOTOGRAPHS

German U-boats had sunk the *Lusitania*, a passenger liner with many American citizens on board, in 1915. The memory of this and the German torpedoing of American cargo ships led the USA to join the Allied fight.

OUR DAY.

The end in sight, 1918

The USA had joined the war in 1917. We nicknamed their lads 'doughboys' and hoped these fresh troops would help us win the war. But when we first got back to France, the Germans seemed to be winning. It wasn't until August 1918 we finally began to push the enemy back and gain ground.

Active Service

Victory, 1918

By the autumn, everyone was exhausted. Enemy soldiers surrendered in their thousands. They just wanted to go home. Germany's allies began to drop out of the war and on 11th November at 11am the fighting stopped. When peace was declared on the front line everything went quiet . . . and then we all went wild, cheering and shaking hands. We'd survived!

Peacetime

After the war I went back to the steelworks; Fred eventually ran a pub near Liverpool. I kept my army spurs as a souvenir and Fred used a brass shell case as the pub's umbrella stand. But the things we'd seen and done and the friends we'd left behind haunted us for the rest of our lives.

Welcome home!

Back home, me and Fred married our sweethearts. We were treated like heroes, but we had learned just how terrible war really was.

SMACK!

Unemployment and a deadly flu epidemic followed the war and I had some run-ins with some Sheffield gangsters. They wanted me to join them! I said 'no' and not very politely – I had to defend myself!

Once a year on Poppy Day, we would meet other veterans at our local war memorial to remember fallen comrades.

All the veterans of World War One have passed away now, including my grandfather and Great-Uncle Fred. But people in many countries still gather on 11th November for Remembrance or Poppy Day to remember those who fought and died in that war, World War Two - and all the wars since then. So on Poppy Day wear a poppy and remember them all.

Charlie was your great-grandfather!

So, he told you his war story when you were little like me?

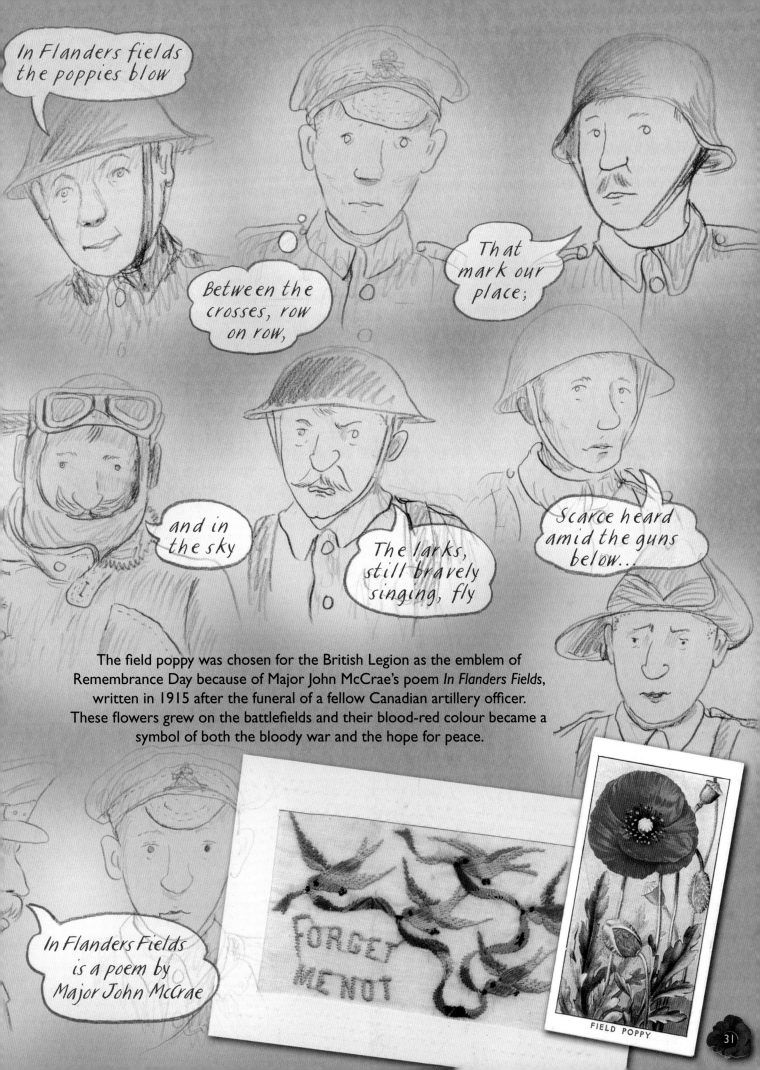

In Flanders fields the poppies blow

Between the crosses, row on row,

That mark our place;

and in the sky

The larks, still bravely singing, fly

Scarce heard amid the guns below...

The field poppy was chosen for the British Legion as the emblem of Remembrance Day because of Major John McCrae's poem *In Flanders Fields*, written in 1915 after the funeral of a fellow Canadian artillery officer. These flowers grew on the battlefields and their blood-red colour became a symbol of both the bloody war and the hope for peace.

In Flanders Fields is a poem by Major John McCrae

FORGET ME NOT

FIELD POPPY

Glossary

Allies – countries united against a common enemy. In World War One, it refers to the countries who fought on the same side as the British.

Artillery – large guns or cannons and the soldiers who use them.

ANZAC – the Australian and New Zealand Army Corps.

Barrage – a prolonged bombardment by artillery guns.

Bombardier – during World War One, a rank in the artillery equivalent to a lance-corporal.

Brigade – in the Royal Artillery during World War One this consisted of individual gun batteries grouped together and commanded by a brigadier.

Casualty – someone killed or wounded in war.

Central Powers – the countries, including Germany and Turkey, who fought against the Allies in World War One.

Front/Front line – where opposing armies face each other in battle.

Limber – the detachable front of a horse-drawn gun carriage, usually consisting of two wheels, axle, pole and an ammunition box, upon which members of the gun crew were seated.

Lord Kitchener – a popular Victorian war hero, who became British Secretary of State for War in 1914. He features on many recruitment posters.

No Man's Land – ground that lay between the opposing armies' trenches and belonged to neither side.

Shells – the ammunition fired by artillery. Some shells contained high explosives, others dozens of round bullets known as shrapnel. Some contained smoke or even poison gas.

Machine gun – a mechanical gun that could fire 500 bullets a minute.

Trench – a ditch dug into the ground for protection.

Veteran – used to describe a person who has fought in war.

A TRIBUTE TO THE ROYAL ARTILLERY

For Charlie and Fred.

Thanks to Charlie, Dad, Mum, Susan, Peter, Mark, Brenda, Richard, Brian, Gwen and Lorraine for sharing precious memories.

First published in 2013 by Franklin Watts, 338 Euston Road, London NW1 3BH; Franklin Watts Australia, Level 17/207 Kent Road, Sydney, NSW 2000.
Text and illustrations © Mick Manning and Brita Granström 2013. Mick and Brita made the illustrations for this book. Find out more at www.mickandbrita.com
Editor: Rachel Cooke; Concept layouts: Mick Manning; Design: Jonathan Hair.
With many thanks to Terry Charman, Amanda Mason, James Taylor and the IWM.
Picture credits: Page 10, image © IWM (HU93771), image reversed for clarity.
Page 4, 22, 24 – IWM archive. All other ephemera from the Manning archives.
A CIP catalogue record is available from the British Library.
Dewey Classification: 904.4. ISBN: 978 1445 11034 9. Printed in China.
Franklin Watts is a division of Hachette Children's Books, an Hachette UK company. www.hachette.co.uk